Begin   to
Spanish

Illustrated by Rebecca Archer

HENDERSON
PUBLISHING PLC
©1992 HENDERSON PUBLISHING PLC

BEGINNER'S GUIDE TO SPANISH

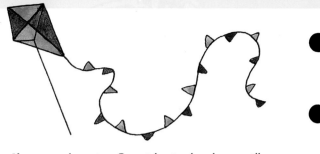

If you are learning Spanish at school you will find that these pages are a great help. They are not meant to be a complete Spanish course but an aid to help you through the early stages of learning the language.

BEGINNER'S GUIDE TO SPANISH

Masculine or Feminine

Remember that, in Spanish, all nouns (words which name things,) are either masculine or feminine. So, there are four words in Spanish for the word 'the', before a noun. The correct word to choose depends on whether the noun is masculine or feminine, singular or plural, like these:

masc. sing.   fem. sing.
el = el libro (the book)   **la** = la casa (the house)

masc. plural   fem. plural
los   **las**

Adjectives (these are describing words) also change their form when they are used with a masculine or feminine noun. Here is an example for you to note:

el libro nuevo   **la casa nueva**
(the new book)   (the new house)

In Spanish, adjectives usually come after the noun.

BEGINNER'S GUIDE TO SPANISH

otro/a other
bonito/a beautiful
bueno/a good
agradable nice
joven young
largo/a long
malo/a bad
pequeño/a small
viejo/a old
nuevo/a new
breve short
guapo/a pretty

BASIC WORDS

Some words are used often in sentences and to ask questions. If you learn them now, you can use them throughout these pages.

Es it is
Qué es eso? what is that ?
Qué es? what is ..?
también also
Hola Hello
Como estas? How are you?
bien fine, well
muy bien very well
bastante enough
bastante bien quite well
no muy bien not very well
muy mal awful

ellos they (masc. or mixed group)
ellas they (fem.)
hay there is, there are
si yes
no no
nunca never
quiza perhaps
algunas veces sometimes

NUMBERS

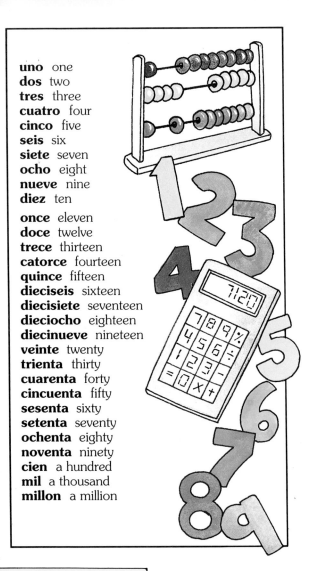

uno one
dos two
tres three
cuatro four
cinco five
seis six
siete seven
ocho eight
nueve nine
diez ten

once eleven
doce twelve
trece thirteen
catorce fourteen
quince fifteen
dieciseis sixteen
diecisiete seventeen
dieciocho eighteen
diecinueve nineteen
veinte twenty
trienta thirty
cuarenta forty
cincuenta fifty
sesenta sixty
setenta seventy
ochenta eighty
noventa ninety
cien a hundred
mil a thousand
millon a million

ALL ABOUT YOU

un muchacho a boy

Yo me llamo Pablo. Como te llamas tu?

la cabeza head	**el dedo** finger
el pelo hair	**el pulgar** thumb
la piel skin	**la mano** hand
el ojo eye	**la pierna** leg
la nariz nose	**la rodilla** knee
la boca mouth	**el dedo del pie** toe
los dientes teeth	**el pie** foot
el pecho chest	**el tobillo** ankle
el brazo arm	

What is he saying?
My name is Pablo.
What's your name?

ALL ABOUT YOU

el pelo rizado curly hair
un flequillo a fringe
el lleva gafas he wears glasses
pelo rubio (claro) fair hair
el perro dog

divertido funny
mover la cola to wag its tail
el gato the cat
hombre the man
ronrronear to purr
simpatico friendly
el bigote moustache

Que edad tienes, Sofia?

Yo tengo ocho anos.

Yo me llamo Marcos. Yo tengo la misma edad que Sofia.

What are they saying?
Pablo: How old are you, Sophie?
Sophie: I am eight years old.
Marcos: My name is Marcos. I am the same age as Sophie.

THE FAMILY

la **familia** the family
el **padre** father
la **madre** mother
la **hermana** sister
el **hermano** brother
el **abuelo** grandfather
la **abuela** grandmother
el **tio** uncle
el **primo** boy cousin
la **prima** girl cousin

What are they saying?
Sophie: Here is my family.
Grandmother: She is my granddaughter.
Aunt: She is my niece. The baby is my nephew.

NOTE: How to say '**my**' ...If you own something single, use **mi**, as in *mi tio* (my uncle). If the noun is plural, like *flores* (flowers), use *mis flores*.

FAMILY EVENTS

el nacimiento birth
la boda wedding
nacer to be born
la novia bride
Mama Mum
el novio bridegroom
Papa Dad
la fiesta party
el regalo gift
el pastel cake
las bodas de oro
golden wedding
la tarta also cake
el globo balloon

What are they saying?
Baby: Waaaah! - it's the same in any language!
Wedding guest: Congratulations
Grandma at birthday party: Happy birthday!
Grandpa at golden wedding: Thank you very much.
Guests at birthday party: Hello.

THINGS PEOPLE DO

el marinero sailor
el soldado soldier
el modelo model

el medico doctor
el comerciante shopkeeper
el cura clergyman
el obrero labourer

el abogado solicitor
el policia policemán
el barrendero dustman

el taxista taxi driver
el camionero lorry driver

THINGS PEOPLE DO

el bombero fireman
el peluquero hairdresser
el granjero farmer

el cocinero cook
el director de banco
bank manager
el cartero postman

el cajero cashier
(male)
la cajera cashier
(female)

el actor actor
la actriz actress
**el director de
orquesta** musical
conductor

THE HOUSE

el tejado roof
la casa house
el edificio block of flats
el piso flat
el balcon balcony
la chimenea chimney

llamar al timbre to ring the bell
el timbre the bell
el vecino neighbour (male)
la ventana window
el portal front door

Yo vivo en esta casa. Donde vives tu?

Yo vivo en un piso.

Yo tambien.

What are they saying?
Pablo: I live in this house. Where do you live?
Sophie: I live in a flat.
Marcos: Me too.

NOTE: How to say '**this**':
For a singular masculine noun, use **este**; a feminine noun is **esta** and a neuter noun is **esto**. **These** is either **estos**, or, for plural feminine nouns - **estas**.

THE KITCHEN

la cocina kitchen
la lavadora washing machine
fregar to wash up
planchar to iron
sucio dirty
fregadera sink
hacer la colada to wash

el armario cupboard
el vaso glass
el pan bread
el te tea
la taza cup
el tenedor fork
el cuchillo knife
la cuchara spoon

Estos platos estan limpios, ahora, Mama.

Bien, Pablo.

What are they saying?
Pablo: These plates are clean, now, Mum.
Mother: Good, Pablo.

THE LIVING ROOM

el cuarto de estar living room

la television television

el video video

las cortinas curtains

el reloj de pared clock

el radiador radiator

el sofa sofa

el sillón armchair
la estufa fire

sentarse junto al fuego to sit by the fire

el libro book
la mesa table
la alfombra carpet
el suelo floor

THE BEDROOM

Buenas noches, Pablo.

Pero, Papa, yo quiero un vaso de agua, por favor.

el dormitorio
bedroom
la cama bed

What are they saying?
Father: Good night, Pablo.
Pablo: But Dad, I'd like a glass of water, please.

el despertador
alarm clock
el bato'n dressing gown
el jersey jumper
la camisa shirt
el pantalon trousers
ir a dormir
to go to sleep
el pijama pyjamas
las zapatillas
slippers
el edredon duvet
dormir to sleep
sonar to dream

THE BATHROOM

el cuarto de baño bathroom
tomar un baño to have a bath
salpicar to splash
la báscula scales
el enchufe plug
el cepillo de dientes tooth-brush
cepillar los dientes to clean your teeth

el javon soap
el grifo the tap
el agua water
caliente hot
frio cold
la pasta de dientes toothpaste
la navaja razor
el espejo mirror
la toalla towel
la ducha shower

THE GARDEN

el jardin garden
hacer el jardin to do the gardening
el cesped lawn
el cuadro flowerbed
el cortacesped lawnmover
la flor flower
la malahierba weed

el árbol tree
el pájaro bird
el invernadero greenhouse
el arbusto bush

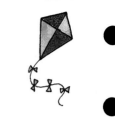

Dónde esta la cometa, Pablo?

Se ha perdido.

Qué pena!

What are they saying?
Marcos: Where is the kite, Pablo?
Pablo: It's lost.
Sophie: What a shame!

GOING SHOPPING

el comercio department store
la escalera el precio the price
el recibo receipt
la clienta female customer

la vendedora female shop assistant
caro/a expensive
el juguete toy
ropa clothes
comprar to buy
mecánica escalator

Ciertamente, Señor.

Quisiera comprar...

What are they saying?
Customer: I would like to buy ...
Assistant: Certainly.

SHOPPING FOR FOOD

carniceria butcher's shop
ultramarinos grocer's shop
pescaderia fishmonger
puesto del mercado market stall
panaderia bakery
hacer cola to stand in a queue
charcuteria delicatessen
pasteleria cake shop
supermercado supermarket

What is she saying?
I have a list and a shopping bag.

UNPACKING THE SHOPPING

el yogurt yoghurt

la barra de pan
long loaf of bread

la leche milk

el arroz rice

la pimienta pepper

el pez fish

los tomates
tomatoes

la manzana apple

los huevos eggs

el vinagre vinegar

las alubias beans

la sal salt

la harina flour

las zanahorias
carrots

las patatas
potatoes

los limones
lemons

AT THE POST OFFICE

correos post office
el paquete parcel
la carta letter
el monedero purse
enviar to send
el bolso handbag

el buzón post box
el dinero money
por avión air mail
el impreso form
el sello stamp

MAKING A PHONE CALL

telefonear to make a telephone call
el teléfono the telephone
marcar el número dial the number
el número de teléfono telephone number

la guia telefónica telephone directory
adios goodbye
colgar to hang up
en caso de emergencia in case of emergency
llamar a la policia call for the police
Dónde esta usted? Where are you?

> **Dígame ..
> Quien esta al
> aparato?**

What is Sophie's Mum saying?
Hello ... Who is speaking?

ASKING THE WAY

Por dónde se va…? Which way is … ?
derecha right
izquierda left
todo derecho straight on
tuerza turn
cojer to take
esta lejos? is it far?
al lado de next to
la calle the street

la primera calle the first street
le segunda calle the second street
la tercera calle the third Street
la iglesia the church
allí over there
perdone excuse me, please …
gracias thank you
de nada you are welcome

Esta la iglesia lejos de aqui?

Despacio, por favor!

Vaya todo derecho hasta la carniceria, despues coja la segunda calle a la izquierda, despues …

What are they saying?
Man: Is the church far from here?
Pablo: Go straight on at the butcher's, then take the second street on the left, then …
Woman: Slowly, please!

AT SCHOOL

parvulario nursery school
escuela primaria primary school
escuela secundaria secondary school
universidad university

la clase classroom
el director headmaster
elcurso course
el alumno boy pupil
la alumna girl pupil
en la escuela at school
leer to read
escribir to write
el patio de recreo playground
el cuaderno exercise book
el plumier pencil case
la regla ruler
el lápiz pencil

AT SCHOOL

el trimestre term
la entrada de curso
beginning of term
el fin del trimestre
end of term
el horario timetable
la ortografía
spelling
la palabra word
la oración sentence
la informática
computer studies
la historia history
la geografía
geography
la química
chemistry
la física physics
la música music
la gimnasia
gymnastics
la computadora
computer
el teclado keyboard

OUT IN THE CAR

la circulación traffic

el coche car

el camión lorry

la bicicleta bicycle

la moto motorbike

rápido fast
lento slow
la autopista motorway
reducir la velocidad to slow down
el embotellamiento traffic jam

el autocar coach

dirección unica one way

los semáforos traffic light

prohibido la entrada no entry

prohibido aparcar no parking

tener una rueda deshinchada to have a flat tyre
estropearse el coche to break down

GOING BY TRAIN

el tren the train
la estación station
la ventanilla de billetes ticket office
el billete ticket
reservar asiento to reserve a seat
el guarda guard

a tiempo on time
coche-cama sleeping car
el rápido express train
el portaequipejes luggage rack
el anden platform
la via track
el horario timetable

AT THE AIRPORT

el aeropuerto
airport
el avion
aeroplane
volar to fly

el equipaje de mano hand luggage

la azafata air hostess

la tienda libre de derechos de aduana duty free shop

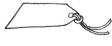

la etiqueta label

la maleta suitcase
nada que declarar nothing to declare
la aduana customs
el aduanero customs official
embarcar to board
el piloto pilot

el carro trolley

el pasaporte passport

TAKING THE FERRY

el puerto port
el ferry ferry
la travesia crossing
el mareo sea sickness
cargar to load
descargar to unload
el agarro the hold
el ancla anchor

la portilla porthole
viajar por barco ravel by boat
la cubierta deck
la chimenea funnel
la pasarela gangway
el capitan captain

AT A CAFE

el camarero waiter
la carta menu
la cuenta bill
la propina tip
la bandeja tray
una coca-cola a cola
un helado ice-cream

un vaso de leche glass of milk
un chocolate hot chocolate
un te con leche tea with milk
un te con limon tea with lemon
el queso cheese
la carne meat
patatas fritas chips
la pizza pizza
la ensalada salad

Que deseas?

Un zumo de naranja y dos limonadas, por favor.

What are they saying?
Waiter: What would you like?
Pablo: An orange juice and two lemonades, please.

FEELING POORLY

las flores flowers
vomitar to be sick
tener un resfriado
to have a cold
estornudar to sneeze
tener fiebre to have a
high temperature
la receta prescription
el comprimido pill
sentirse mejor
to feel better

Hola. Tienes dolor de estómago?

No, me duele la cabeza

What are they saying?
Sophie: Hello, Marcos. Have you got stomach-ache?
Marcos: No, I have a headache.

THE TIME OF DAY

la mañana morning
el mediodia
afternoon
la tarde evening
mediodia noon
medianoche
midnight

Qué hora es? What
time is it?
Es la una en punto
It is one o'clock
**Son las cinco en
punto** It is five o'clock

**son las siete menos
cuarto** quarter to
seven
**son las siete menos
diez** ten to seven
son las siete y cinco
five past seven
**son las siete y
cuarto** quarter past
seven
**son las siete y
media** half past seven

**Son las ocho de la
noche** It is eight
o'clock in the evening

THE WEATHER

el invierno winter

la primavera spring

el verano summer

el otoño autumn

esta lloviendo it's raining
hace frio it's cold
la lluvia rain
trueno thunder
relampago lightening
arco-iris rainbow
granizo hail

la nieve snow
tengo calor I'm hot
hay niebla It's foggy
el viento the wind
hace viento It's windy
el sol brilla the sun is shining
escarcha frost

Hace bueno.

Qué tiempo hace?

What are they saying?
Sophie: What's the weather like?
Mother: It's fine.

THE DAY AND THE DATE

Qué dia es tu compleaños?

Mi compleaños es el veintiuno de abril.

enero January
febrero February
barzo March
abril April
mayo May
junio June
julio July
agosto August
septiembre.. September
octubre October
noviembre November
diciembre December

domingo Sunday
lunes Monday
martes Tuesday
miercoles Wednesday
jueves Thursday
viernes Friday
sabado Saturday

What are they saying?
Marcos: What is the date of your birthday?
Sophie: My birthday is the twenty-first of April.

THE DAY AND THE DATE

el dia day
la semana week
el mes month
el año year
hoy today
ayer yesterday
mañana tomorrow
antes-de-ayer the day before yesterday
pasado mañana the day after tomorrow
la semana siguiente next week
el dia siguiente the following day
el próximo viernes next Friday
el uno de mayo the first of May
el dos de noviembre the second of November

AROUND THE WORLD

el mundo the world
el norte north
el sur south
el oeste west
el este east
el polo norte
North Pole
el polo sur
South Pole
el país country
el continente
continent
Gran Bretaña
Great Britain
Fracia France
Suiza Switzerland

Alemania Germany
Los paises bajos
Holland
Italia Italy
España Spain
Los estados unidos
America
India India
China China
Nueva Zelanda
New Zealand
Australia Australia
America del sur
South America
Rusia Russia

AT THE BEACH

en la playa at the seaside
castillo de arena sandcastle
el balde bucket
la pala spade
la roca rock
el cangrejo crab
la concha shell
la gaviota seagull
la ola wave

nadar to swim
la playa beach
chapotear to paddle
patinar sobre las olas to go windsurfing
las gafas de sol sunglasses

What are they saying?
Pablo: How much is an ice-cream?
Man: Forty pesetas

AT THE ZOO

el zoo the zoo
animal salvaje wild animal
la cebra zebra
la jirafa giraffe

la foca bebe baby seal
el pingüino penguin

el leon lion
el tigre tiger

el camello camel
el avestruz ostrich

oso polar polar bear

el elefante elephant
el colmillo tusk
el mono monkey

ON THE FARM

la verja gate
el trigo wheat
cosechar to harvest
la oveja sheep
el perro pastor
sheepdog

la pieza field
el granjero farmer
el cerdo pig
el granero barn
la vaca cow
el cordero lamb

Todavia no, Pablo. Dentro de una semana.

Es tiempo de segar, abuelo.

What are they saying?
Pablo: Is it harvest, Grandad?
Grandad: Not yet, Pablo - in a week's time.

COLOURS

As a colour is an adjective, it may be masculine (often ending in 'o'), or feminine (ending in 'a'), to agree with the noun it accompanies. That is why there is a choice of ending for some colours. Where there is no choice, the colour can be either masculine or feminine.

el color colour
brillante bright
apagado/a dull
palido/a pale
oscuro/a dark
rojo/a red
azúl blue
verde green
morado/a purple
naranja orange
negro/a black
blanco/a white
gris grey
amarillo/a yellow

MEASUREMENTS

la altura height
medir to measure
el metro metre
la anchura width
la largura length

el volumen volume
un litro a litre
medio litro half a litre

el peso weight
medio kilo half a kilo

la forma shape

el círculo circle

el triangulo triangle

el cuadrado square

HOBBIES

yo hago punto
I knit

yo toco el piano
I play the piano

yo pinto I paint

**yo miro la
televisión** I like to
watch T.V.

me gusta cocinar
I like to cook

**me gusta el
deporte**
I like sport

yo bailo I dance

yo leo libros
I read books

EATING WITH FRIENDS

sirvete Help yourself
Quieres más?
Would you like more ...?
He comido suficiente, gracias
Thank you, I have enough
Esta muy rico It's delicious

Me puedes pasar por favor Please pass me ...
que te divertas
Have fun, enjoy yourself
está sobre la mesa
It's on the table
haber comido bien
I have had a good meal

Gracias, tengo mucha hambre.

Que aproveche.

What are they saying?
Mother: Enjoy your meal
Sophie: Thank you. I'm really hungry.

POINTS TO REMEMBER

The
The clue to whether a spanish word is masculine
or feminine lies in the word for 'the'. '**El**' is
used before masculine nouns and '**la**' before
feminine ones. This is for singular nouns.. In
the plural, use '**los**' for masculine nouns, and
'**las**' for feminine ones.

A or An
'A' or 'an' is '**un**' with masculine nouns, and
'**una**' before feminine ones.

My and Your
mi my
nuestro/a our
tu your (singular)
vuestro/a your (plural)
su his, her, its
su their

POINTS TO REMEMBER

It

In Spanish, there isn't one word for 'it' - again it depends on whether the 'it' is masculine or feminine. 'Ellos' and 'ellas' are the plural versions.

Some

The word to use for 'some' is '**algo**' for a singular quantity, like *some water* but '**algunos/as**' in the plural, like *some girls*.

PRONUNCIATION

This is a guide towards making the right sound.
It is better, though to copy the accent of a
Spanish person, if you can find one to teach
you.

a ... sounds like the 'a' in *far*

e ... sounds like the 'e' in *fern*

i ... sounds like the 'ee' in *see*

o .. sounds like the 'a' in *ball*

u ... sounds like the 'oo' in *root*

PRONUNCIATION

c in front of an 'i' or an 'e' sounds like *th* in *three*

ch sounds like *ch* in *chocolate*

g + a,o,u sounds like *g* in *go*

g + e,i sounds like *j*

j sounds like *ch* in the Scottish word, *loch*

n sounds like the first *n* in *onion*

qu sounds like the *k* in *kite*

h is always silent